DOPPELGÄNGSTER

Self-Portraits in a Funhouse Mirror

ALSO BY JEFFREY CYPHERS WRIGHT

Translust

Charges

Employment of the Apes

Two
(with Yvonne Jacquette)

Take Over
(Introduction by Allen Ginsberg)

Over the Years, An Oral History of Harlem

All in All
(Preface by Alice Notley)

Walking on Words

Drowning Light

Flourish

The Name Poems

October Centerfold
(with Nathaniel Hester)

Triple Crown, Three Crowns of Sonnets

Blue Lyre

Party Everywhere

Radio Poems

Fake Lies

By and By, Birthday Poems

The Mean Poems

Erato's Inbox

3-Zero, Turning 30
(Editor, with Elinor Nauen)

Over the Years, Oral Histories from Harlem
(Editor)

DOPPELGÄNGSTER

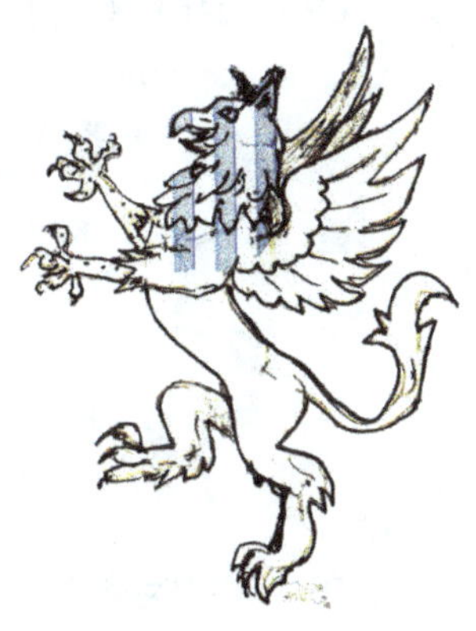

Self-Portraits in a Funhouse Mirror

by

Jeffrey Cyphers Wright

MadHat Press
MadHat Incorporated
PO Box 422, Cheshire, MA 01225

The Library of Congress has assigned
this edition a Control Number of
2023935277

ISBN 978-1-952335-58-7 (paperback)

Words by Jeffrey Cyphers Wright
Cover image & interior artwork by Jeffrey Cyphers Wright
Book design by Lori Ortiz

www.MadHat-Press.com

First Printing
Printed in the United States of America

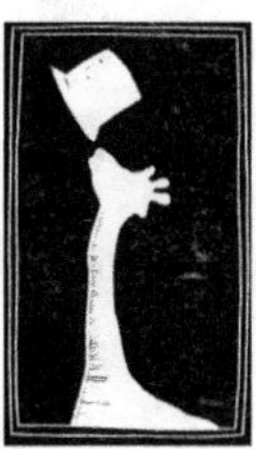

ARTWORKS

CONTENTS

PART I: SHIVERING IN UTOPIA

PART II: STRETCHING SILENCE

FOREWORD

Though fruitless, our search through the grass quests on, the lawn jockey still eggs us forward. Or was that backward? Sideways? Perpendicular?

Go ask Alice.

If a guide-book existed for this oddly familiar terrain, it might wonder at all one can do with 14 lines, as this book does. This book lifts your rod in a rain-storm, letting "Lightning strike lightning" and "bolts us to the sky" with what sparkles inside.

In whatever direction we've ventured (ask the Cheshire Cat), we learn the author, like Cupid, is "a disciple of Venus." The feel of the arrow's wound is felt in the very first poem.

In this house, the mirror's chief distinction isn't its concave or convex shape, but its fun nature. "Fun" is through the glass to this sensibility, its quarry as old as Sappho's lyre.

Through this glass one goes poem by poem. No set meters measure the walk and Wright keeps rearranging his 14 line stairway. There will be no regular rhyme scheme, no A-B-A-B, but somehow these lines remind us why we read poetry at all; not for meter, rhyme or the proper response to the day's gruesome slab of history, whatever it is.

We read for the Beauty in it and that's all we'll ever know, or need to know on Earth. And here, it shines back from this funhouse mirror on the reader's capacity to fashion the pictures found in these lines. Imagine that!

Writing this foreword got me to thinking about the world so well represented in *Midsummer Night's Dream* and Lewis Carrol. Herrick also did some nice work in this area. He may be the poet of "daintiness." Anyway, these poems brought me into this kind of consciousness and it's a great place to try and think from. This poetry gets into a very similar place, but it keeps a sort of street savvy wit about it which keeps it from getting too syrupy. There's a lot for poets to learn here. As the Bard instructed:

> *Go, Philostrate,*
> *Stir up the Athenian youth to merriments,*
> *Awake the pert and nimble spirit of mirth.*

And banish a roof erected to shelter us from the rain, because it blocks out the Sun. It's hard to defend Beauty with a capital B. I can't really call myself an atheist because I believe in it. It's the purity of it and this poetry is pure.

—James Ruggia

PART I

SHIVERING IN UTOPIA

Parachuting from the Sun

Some people live for money—
some live for fame.
You well up, Honey,
you're an island bound by rain.

Some people live forever.
Some move beyond the frontier.
You carry me over rivers
where stars bathe in desire.

You're going to take
driving lessons
& I'm going to be your car.
No permit necessary.

Lightning striking lightning
bolts us to the sky.

All That

Not everyone can carry the weight of the world.
—REM

I see myself as a raven in the sun,
a disciple of Venus,
a saddle cinched around a nightmare.
Sure, I do my share of damage,
but in the drip roar, you are my waterfall.
A whirring harvester of mini-gods
holding it together
in spite of thrash warnings.
A burning ladder emblazons our flag,
planted on a liberated playground
near the albatross graveyard.
Besides all that, I'm a guest of Miss Align.
I see myself as an Eastern Hornbeam.
Not everyone's nailed to a crosswind.

Doppelgängster

Wolf behind the wheel.
What dudes we be,
skimming masks of glass
across a bourbon sea.
The mirror smoking
all my weed.
Terminal desire
in the oracle flare.
Selling fiddles to infidels
under withering fire.
Silent heat
wrings jade from me:
these lines, raked
like coals from the sun.

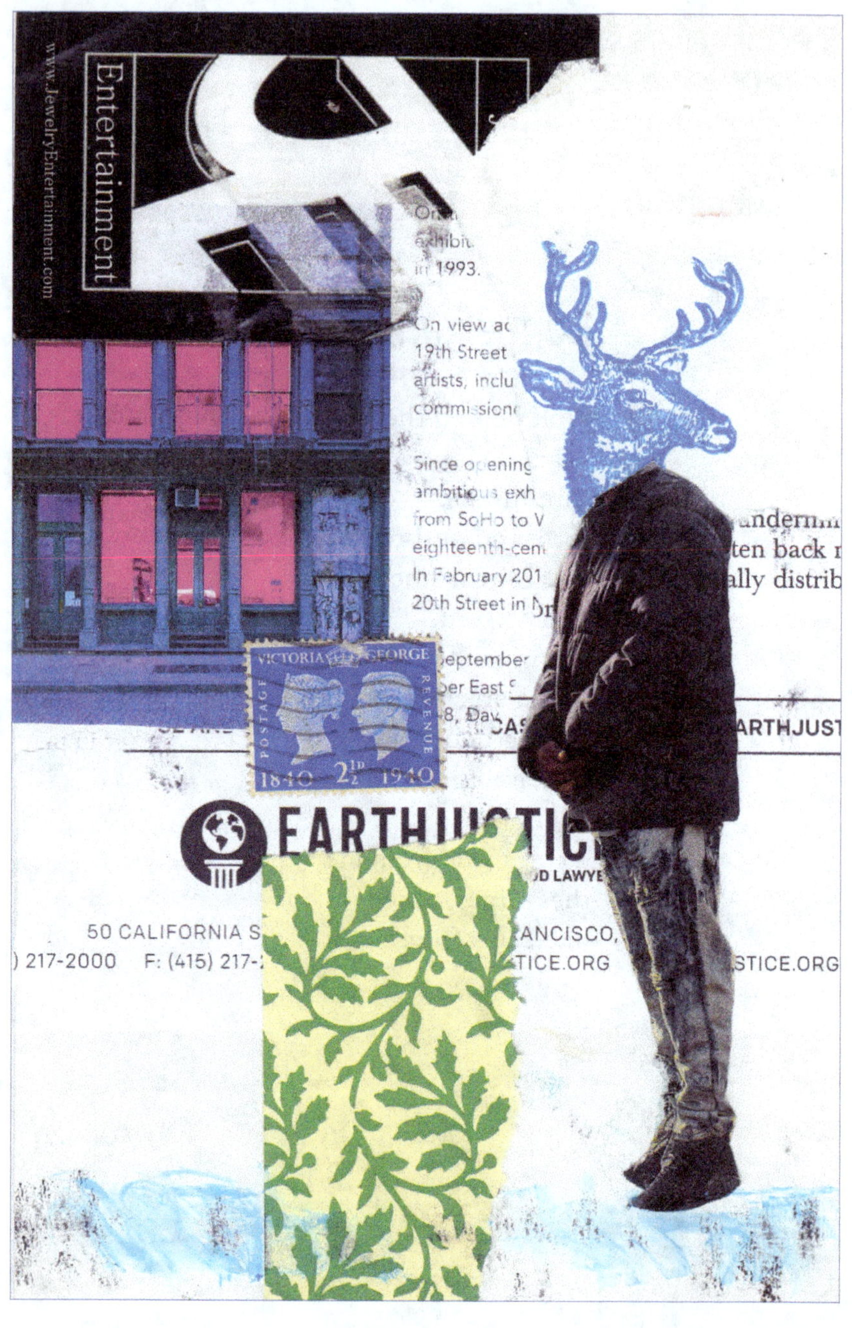

www.JewelryEntertainment.com
Entertainment
in 1993.
On view ac
19th Street
artists, inclu
commissione
Since opening
ambitious exh
from SoHo to V
eighteenth-cent
In February 201
20th Street in
September
ber East
8, Day
VICTORIA GEORGE
POSTAGE
REVENUE
1840 2½D 1940
EARTHJUSTICE
ARTHJUST
underm
ten back
ally distrib
50 CALIFORNIA S
ANCISCO,
) 217-2000 F: (415) 217-
TICE.ORG
STICE.ORG

Blue

Blue, I want you blue.
BLUE FULL OF LIGHT BREATH
with dignity (and liberty) for all.
Blue Power.
Blue Money.
Blue Waves of Blue Energy.
When they go low, we get high.
You can say that again,
Chief Blue-in-the-Face.
Blue polar bear ghosts racing past.
Blue ink running down the street
in blue diamond rain.
Blue jobs. Blue fangs.
Blue change, changing everything.

Dancing with Fire

From my mother I inherited
easy grace and savoir faire.
My father blessed me with
a quick wit and sticky Irish ire.
Night arrives in its velvet car,
seducing the vain weather.

I wear your ring and let you
rub my good luck charm.
You think you'll have the soup.
We are mobilizing for the coup.
Confounded by profoundness,
who can help fill in the blanks?

I dream of Hippolyte's niteclub,
dancing with fire in my blood.

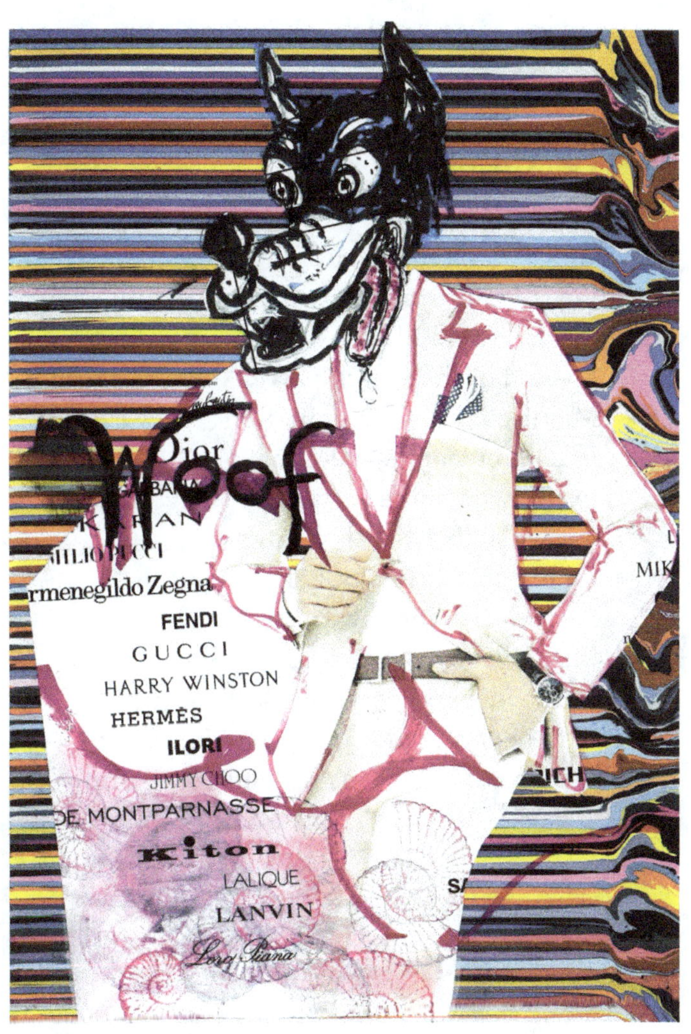

Woof
Dior
rmenegildo Zegna
FENDI
GUCCI
HARRY WINSTON
HERMÈS
ILORI
JIMMY CHOO
DE MONTPARNASSE
Kiton
LALIQUE
LANVIN
Loro Piana

Divining Rod

Go ye, fetch the mentor of the minotaur.
Whistle for wisdom's wishlist.
If lips could kill, I'd work on my will.
I would dj the search party.
Making room for rumination
is a Herculean task. Let us
twist away in the extinction foray
with friends from the fringe.
Joking about the funny bones of Elba.
Bengals playing the Titans.
Mo spills my Old Fashioned—
words in a notebook get sloshed
like we *almost* did. Well, you *did*, cousin.
A path runs away inside your moccasin.

Étude No. 69

At Hillary's party, windows all
open wide. Williamsburg Bridge,
a black hulk with a red eye,
breaches the raggedy skyline.
Right off, I lie, telling Brooke,
"Neil knows 'Letter to Parsifal.'"
We all sing "Summertime."
Neil says he had pickled herring
for lunch and I say I had creamed
herring, adding, "My favorite
president was Herring Truman."
And the Ouija board outs you—
says your favorite number is 69.
I'll be a flute and you, the wind.

Fake Lies

The donor class is warping the loom.
Domination is damnation.
Defiance is a shortcut to *de-finance*.
We have to scrap for all that's left.
Make of your suffering, charms.
The best things are free (like me),
but cocktails cost an arm and a liege.

Sipping a Tombstone at Suffolk Arms,
we revel without a causality.
Nothing to it. Just drip your lips
into mine. Drive me insane.
Ferrari in a fire lane in a sanctuary city,
racing toward a burning eternity.
Only with you do I win by giving in.

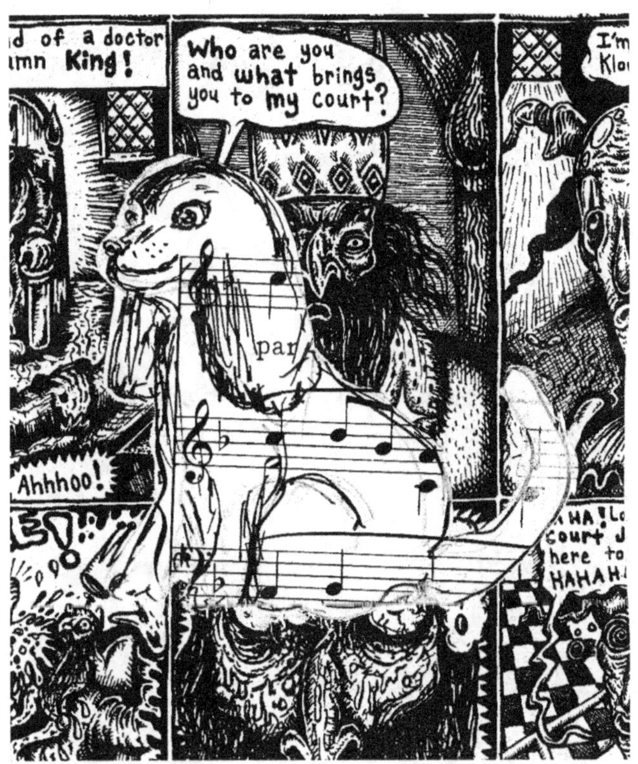

d of a doctor
mn King!
Who are you and what brings you to my court?
I'm
Klo
par
Ahhhoo!
HA! Lo
court
here to
HAHAH

Pinocchio's Birthday

It's Rumble Whirl versus Fenwick Hall
in the 7th at Saratoga today.
Bees are busy clover-hopping,
quilting the humming field.

I am not a real boy it seems,
but sometimes you are a living doll.
And this, I suppose, is a real poem
I'm managing to scrawl.

Camptown Races, 5 miles long,
Ode to Doo Dah Day.
Pegasus kicks dark clouds over Kingston.
Tonight, we drink white lightning.

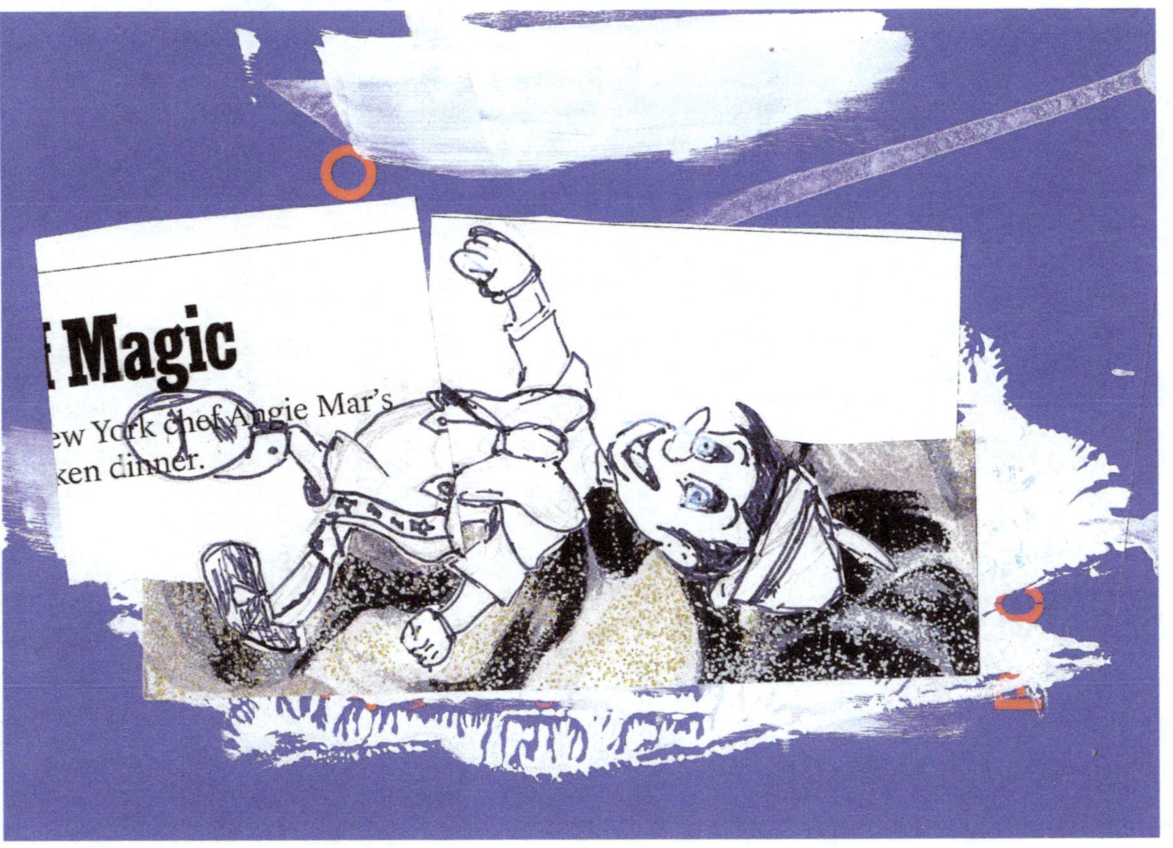
Magic
ew York chef Angie Mar's
ken dinner.

Mistressism

Let us now surround ourselves with pleasure,
electric flanks of silk
fueled by lightning.

Wearing boxing gloves in the war on boredom,
wearing your heart on a shield,
you walk like an oasis stalking paradise.
DRUM ROLE

Wild still your blood pounds,
munching on the tail end of infinity.

Sentenced to sit on a burning throne,
all you know is all you own.
Blackberries, white wine, trombones…

The new moon is back sporting a fat lip.
Where does your hairy eye go when you cum?

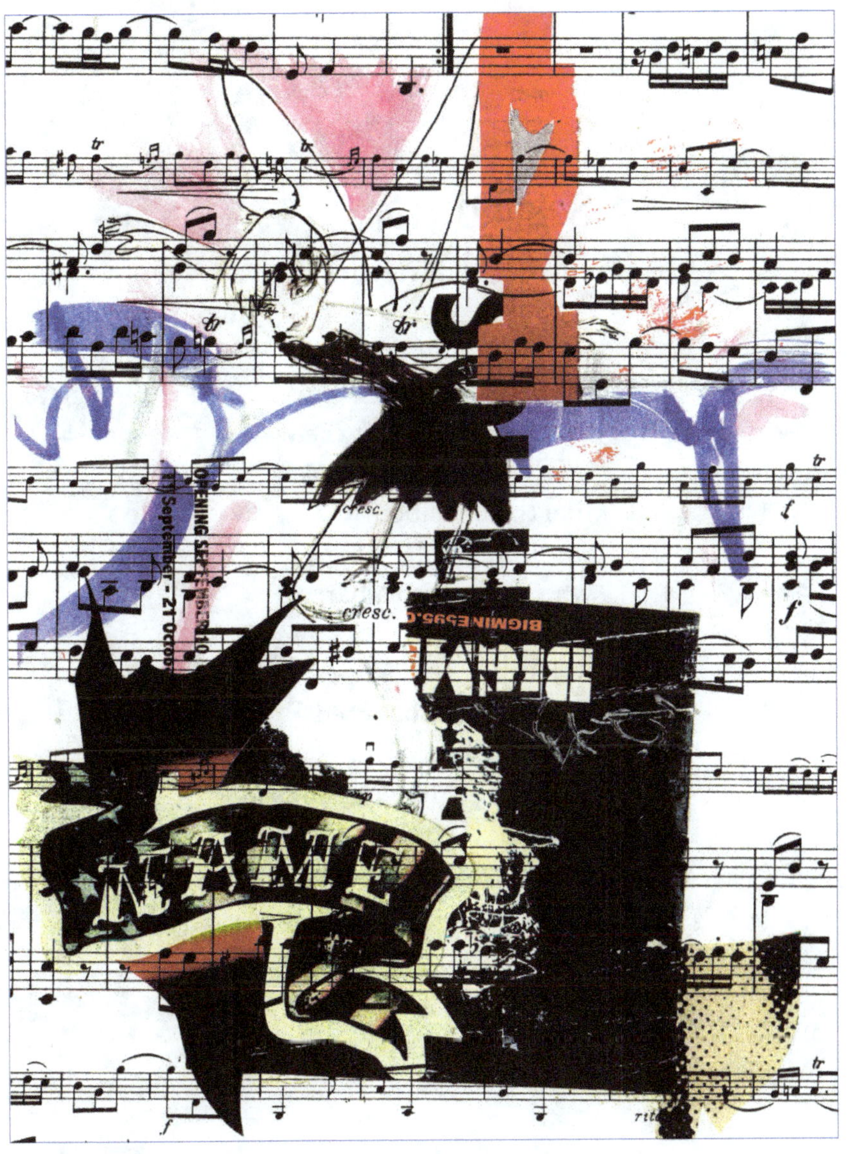
cresc.
cresc.
NAME

Self-Portrait as a Snowman

I smile. I sing. I babysit.
My words bolster the weak.
To the lost, I point the way.
To the infirm, I tell jokes
like the one about
the albino polar bear
who walks into a bar.
The bartender asks,
"What'll it be, *Redeye?*"
For this am I honored
and for honor we live.
Another year spun 'round
the sun. If you can't
find magic, make some.

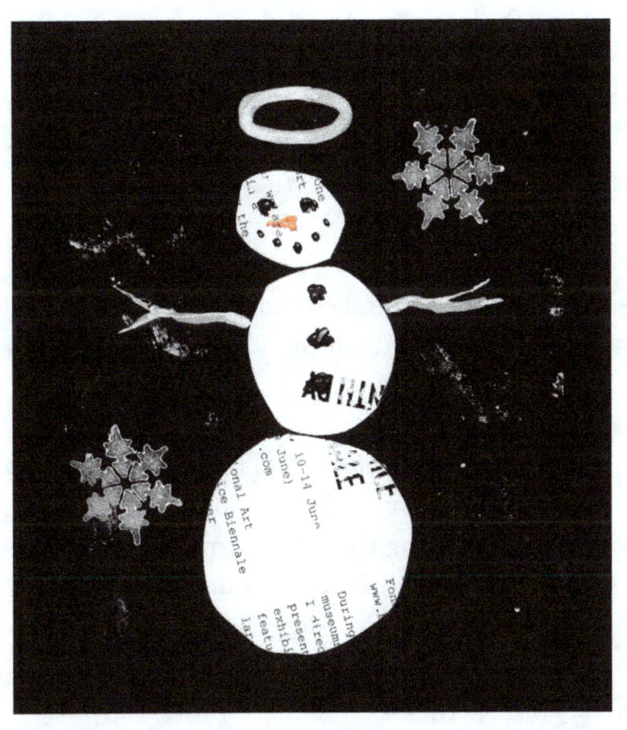

Truth vs. Meaning

It's almost true, that before I became
Mr. Universe, I was a nobody.
I performed for orphans behind the front.
I did tricks designed to evade destiny

by testing the interface between
the inner life and the *outré*.
We all know about predictability,
speaking of which:

November is packing its brown valise.
It's tired of my bad direction.
Embarrassing the set designer.
If I knew how to act, I wouldn't act up.

I might know the difference between
a burning fire engine and a naked siren.

Classic Madhattan

Use locally sourced rye whiskey.
Today we are using Defiant from upstate.
Play Nina Simone's "Memphis in June."

Pit three Bing cherries and put them
into a chilled tumbler.
Add 2 oz chilled Defiant rye

Add ½ oz chilled sweet vermouth
Add 1 oz chilled tart cherry juice
2–3 dashes of Bitters

Today we're using "The Bitter Truth."
Strain over ice. It's an instant classic
like you. Making it up as we go.

It's Manhattan in June.
The fountains titter over their fortunes.

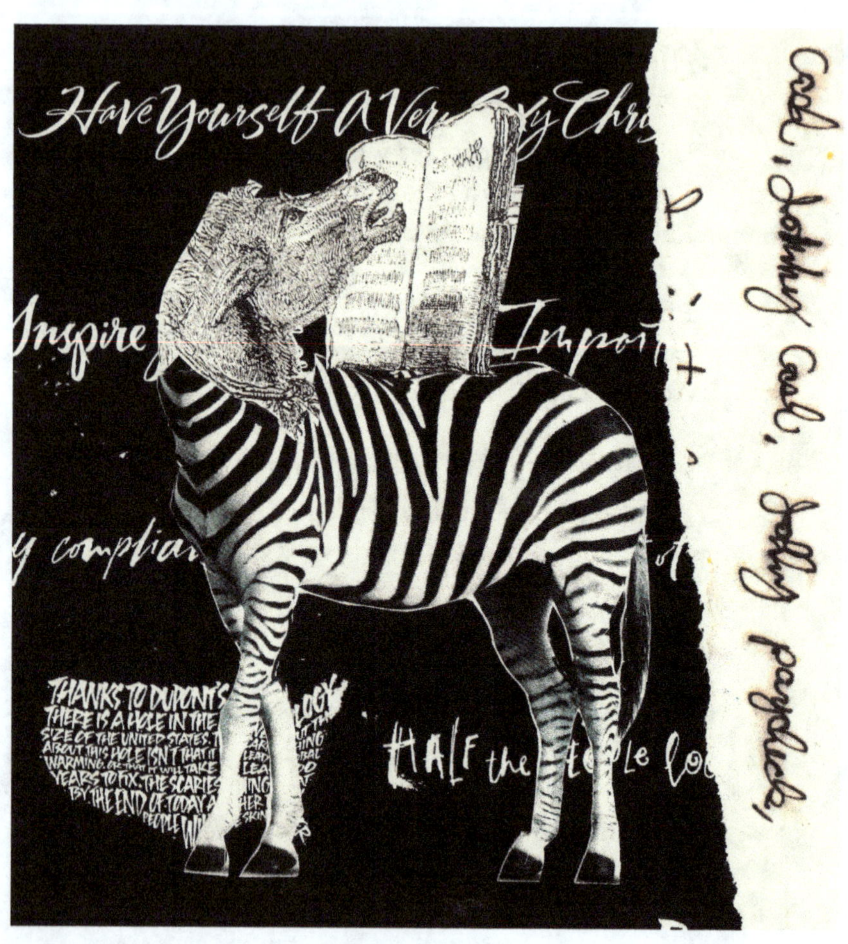

Have Yourself A Very
Inspire
THANKS TO DUPONT'S
THERE IS A HOLE IN THE
SIZE OF THE UNITED STATES.
ABOUT THIS HOLE ISN'T THAT IT
WARMING.
YEARS TO FIX. THE SCARIES
BY THE END OF TODAY A
HALF the

Secretary of Dissent

Does the word *dossier* scare you?
In the future everyone has one.
They are kept at the Ministry
of Memory Reconstruction

and Normative Corrections.
Abnormal is the new normal!
Global warming is hokum!
What rhymes with orange skin?

Putin! "Ha ha ha."
There's a new circus in town.
So it's like, the howler monkey
and the wolf had a baby. "Ha ha."

The problems of the world
are ours, but we are never alone.

Build a Wall

I

Let's build a wall using
dumped steel from China,
radioactive waste from Japan,
dead journalists from Russia
and bankers from Iceland.
Let's use Tokay bottles
from the Pine Ridge Reservation.
Let's use bleeding zombie eyes
from Bollywood.
Let's use confederate flags.
Let's all of us, unite in spirit,
and all that is noble inside,
and let us stand tall, on top
of our wall, when it is done,
and laugh until we die.

II

We'll build our wall a block
at a time, using ivory.
Rhino horns. Coral reefs.
Refugees washed up.
Let's build our wall
using child labor.
Let's build our wall
out of red ties. Lipstick.
Vats of sperm whale sperm.
Let's build this wall
on melting icebergs.
Let's build it on sand,
for the sandman cometh.
Can you spare a tire?

III

Oh, great wall. We will
absolve ourselves in thee
and thy electronic veil,
thy curtain of surveillance.
Wall made of hamburgers.
Wall made of dog whistles,
using parts of junked hearts.
The Mofo of all walls.
Riding shotgun on a hearse
lost in the place of yetness.
Walled city on a hillbilly.
Eyeless dolls blinking.
Wall of spookhouse mirror fear.
Wall of worms, made of tears.

Locker Room

Who haunts the ghost?
Who walks the dog?
Who mocks the turtle?
Who listens to a log?

Live by the penis, etc.
Shivering in Utopia.
Slow smoking October sky.
Pave the road with lyres.

Orpheus sleeping
with one eye weeping.
Who would trap a fowl?
A special suckerfice.

Anyway, I love you.
Grab 'em by the antenna.

Art of the Duel

Dear Cupid, I love your mom
but my cart is full. (Alas.)

A glass of wind sips afternoon.
Everything passes like gas.

I parody Pierrot's parrot, unable
to separate meaning from mien.

"Siri, what's your favorite drink?"
"I thirst for knowledge," she says.

Bats descend on the West Wing.
My nomadic skin crawls.

You don't have to fight dirty to win.
Sacrifice is all we're asking for.

Meet me at the sun's stump. Take
ten paces, turn, and fire the boss.

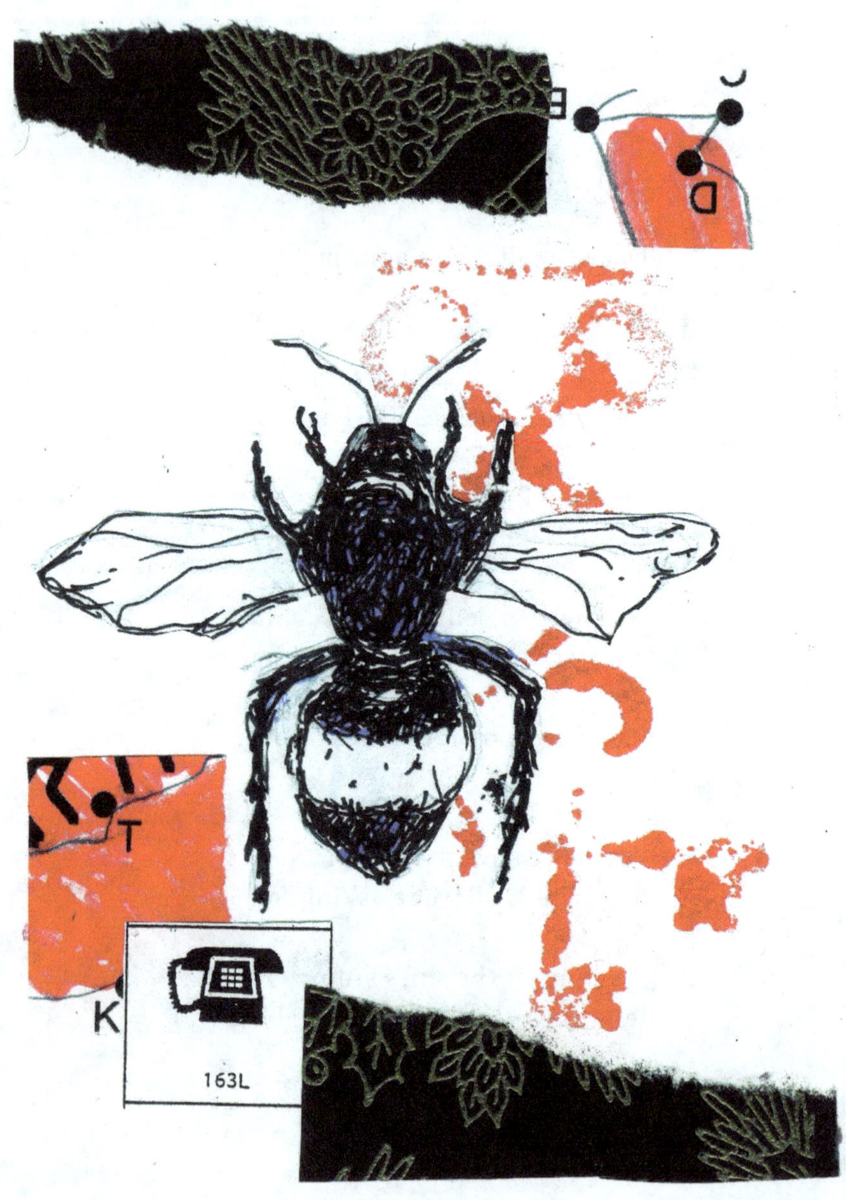
D
T
K
163L

Flight Manual

for Barry Wallenstein

Obey the wind when it waggles your wings.
Blue-streak curse when you get hurt.
Lie when the dice are more loaded than you.

Live like tomorrow owes you a silver dollar.
Love like fog hugging the river, before
dawn's red cap ushers in a separate agenda.

Join a chorus of flame-throwers all aimed
at the same outcome—a silver-tailed comet
that shows up in your eyes when you stare

at the ghost we're seamlessly laying out
to take the place of forever and its rabble horde,
lost in the crossroads of your place or mine.

Try hard to find a way to be found.
The diamonds we cut don't hoard any shine.

Rough Patch

Old dandelions tip
white hats to the wind.
What's above, calls
on what's below.
ROADWORK AHEAD
There's nothing any more
between us and it's too much.
I'm going nuts.
Take me to the wetlands
where you abuse
the heart of absence.
We were toys in Babeland.
Ah, lover. Teach me to beg.
Give my shadow back.

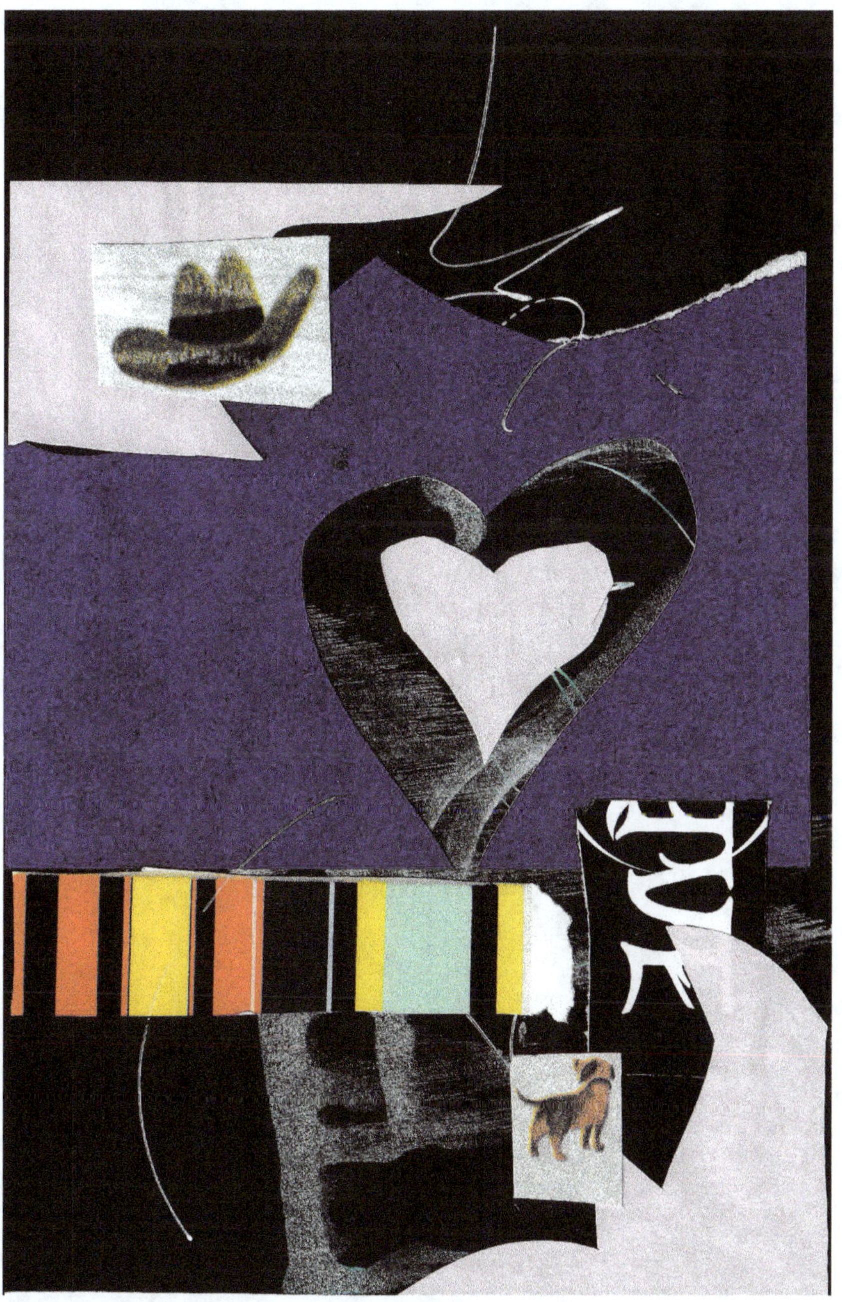

Make It Happen

Laughter sifts the wind.
Eyes kiss the light.
Let me enroll you
in a hypnagogic state.
What's up with that?
You hold the dust
in your oven mitt.
You adjust the motes
circling all the routes
of escape. One wing
is a myth. One wing
is a mouth. Surrounding
you, so to speak.
"There is no plan B."

How to Live with Yourself

There are only two sins—banality and venality.
They are not like revenge, hot red pokers.
Jealousy, with its long snoot.
Sloth, killing me softly with its lips.
Vanity—dynamite in a vise.
Lust racing across the mudflats.
Rage is too honest. Fear is pointless.
Procrastination is a rabid possum.
Perfection is a crime waiting for permission.
Regret, a pain in the behind. Sure,
I've been a sucker for love, but only because
you're madc of colored sugar
and the moon is your babysitter.
Take a fool's advice—don't beat your heart.

Imp Lotion

I will call you Aztec Heartbeat.
Mission Accomplice. Hurt Ban.
We'll go to the Beekman
and have an Old Fashioned
with Dottie. Who is aptly named.
Life is hard and so am I.
Dreadnaught. Jiggernaut.

You can call me Easy Fingers.
Ruby Tingler. Muskrat Love.
I don't know how to spend time
so I waste it. Forgive me, Fortuna,
for I have already forgiven you.
Rub my lamp with nothing
but devotion to our implosion.

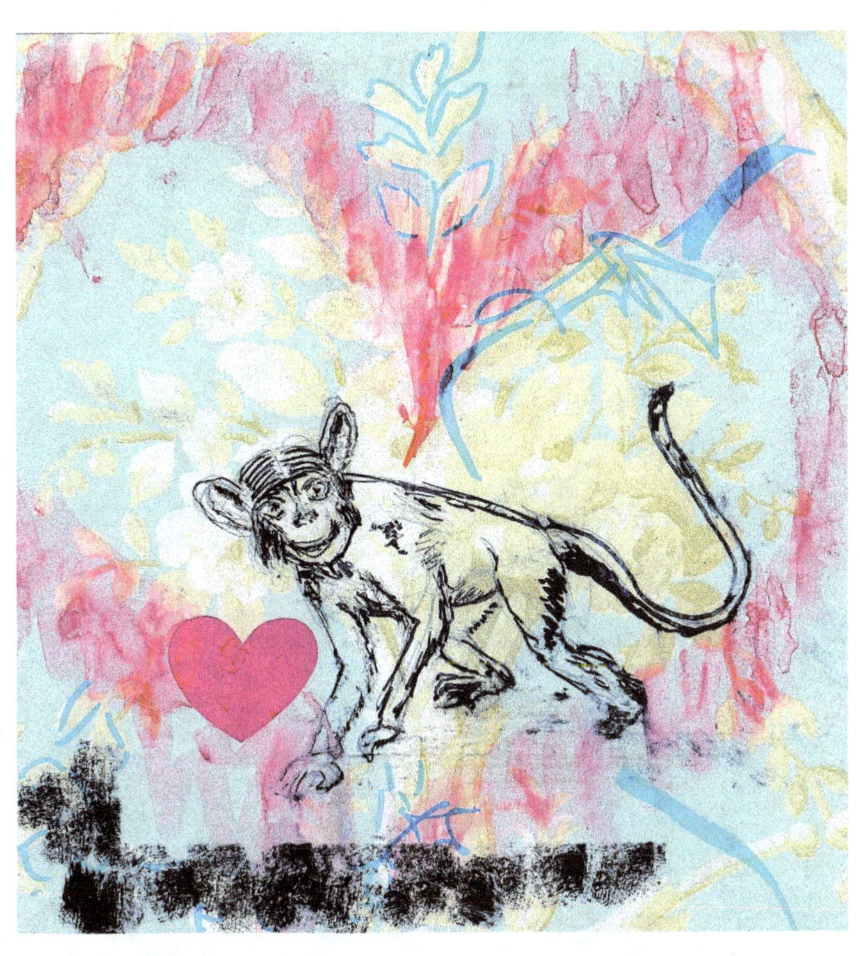

Santa as a Young Viking

My mother was a Viking, my father a Dane.
My aunt was a stitch, my uncle a thane.

My province lies north of tomorrow.
The bone-white landscape simulating peace.

Once I built an imaginarium.
And the Magi still come.

I'll give you a tip. Review your stocks.
I'm going to need a lot of coal this year.

And don't be asking for silver or gold,
titles or deeds, awards or absolution.

I bring only belief. Belief in love
and its veil of covalence.

I live with some elves now.
We make toys for fun, out of resolution.

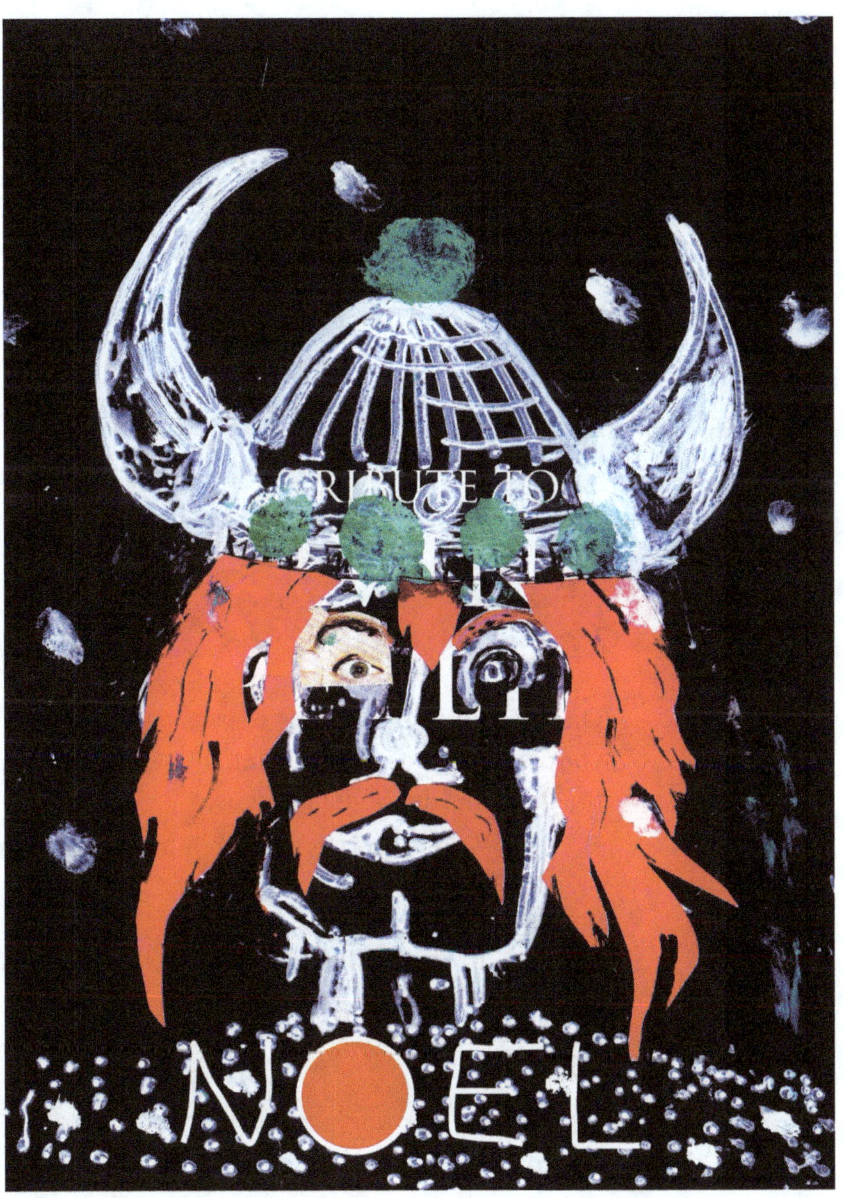
NOEL

Tilt

TV anchors gab about binge-
watching, riots, and tattoos.
The machine has a boo boo.
We are in some deep doo doo.

Blue jays peck red berries,
91 degrees and I am a sap.
Jupiter's ma pushes old news:
It's more fun with someone.

Okay, steeple chaser, let's see
your stuff. Here's a hot ticket
for the Tingling Sisters Circus.
It's time to give the frog a kiss.

On mercy's wings we arrive.
Moving in where silence sings.

Laughing Matter

October rattles, dry stalks
clacking evening's prattle.
I'm not even jealous of you, Time,
with your hand in my pocket.
Ink poured into a coffin.
The moon dressed in white satin.

The empire shambles along.
The gladiators are not all glad.
Here in the pang fortress
I hide among the angel's fangs,
like gum being chewed on
but not spitten or swallowed.

Let me show you, before we go,
how to draw a word out of a sword.

Gambling with the Past

Your nightgown's rosette has faded.
The whiff of courage and oats, faint.
How fond I've grown of all our ties.
A load of free tears waits
at the end of your reign. Even now
I catch the sky stealing a blue crayon.

You're cute saying "collyflower."
We see The Factory at the museum.
We watch a preview of oblivion.
Search Injun.
We were all we did to get better at this.
We were head ushers at the hip parade.

Your fortune cookie says: "Eat me."
A red carpet follows us like a tongue.

Spreading the Wealth

Each snowflake is the king of wind,
diving and rising by command,
until landing on snowdrops
who bow pale lavender heads.

You go back and forth between
being blind and seeing into my heart,
forever on trial in love's court.

But you always come out on top.
Like snow. Embarrassingly beautiful
in your intent at least.
You never promise to compromise
and we are louder than allowed
syncing the dream bundle
with full rounds of empty wonder.

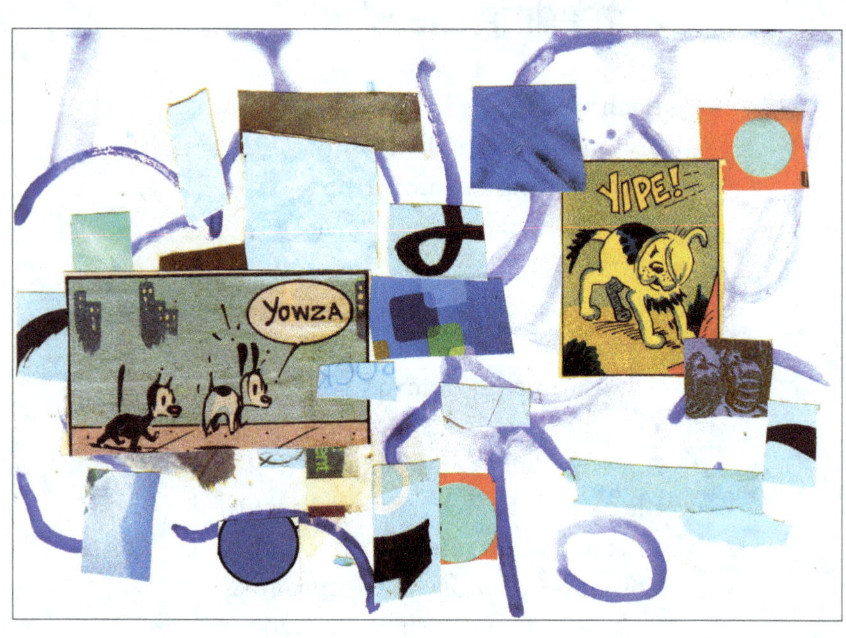
YOWZA
YIPE!

Trained Wreck

I always led from the back of our class.
My pals were yankee rebels. It wasn't
our thing to be official. We never
went out for varsity. I wanted an A-plus
in bra unhooking and slango.
And pencil drumming. After a point
teachers would say, "You can do better."
I could be class clown or
wear a sanctioned crown.
When Santa, and then Jesus, bailed
the changes unrolled, folding suddenness
into a haphazard master plan—
blue footprints skirting disaster.
The hounds always run ahead of the horn.

Four Fire Day

Dad worried that the youth weren't
going to pick up the slack.
It bothered him that there were
more rock 'n' roll bands than scientists.
I said you have to follow the bonds
taloned to the sky, even unto the last
ditches of the dying sun agasp in the west.

Endless knowledge is noble, I agreed,
but pointless except in its application.
If I were king, I'd give free singing lessons.
When no one has a job, they'll still
have a voice. A song is a torch.
There are four fires out of control today.
Would you rather discover or be discovered?

Temple of Jupiter

Hello, Sibyl. Old fortune teller.
Dusk in its blue taxi
weeps at your endless agony.
Poetry should be grief, not grievances.
I come to hear your prophecy—
how the world is shrinking
like your cage of immortality.

Show me how to convert the useless.
The graceless and wasteful.
The northern half of a southern laugh.
Reveal to us how to yearn so purely
we turn into hollow light.
"Please ask for assistance."
Let me chew on your fat dreams.

The Missing Lynx

Uncle Google won't tell me who I am.
Sandra Day O'Connor can't recall our date.
Jimmy Hoffa waits for me under a bridge.
The Mormon Tabernacle Choir is crying
over my unvirtual reality.
Vladimir has accessed my precedent.

There will never be another pure moment.
Ghosts outnumber us, demanding equality.
Daily have I dallied
and watched my options dwindle.
Now I kindle darkness.
Nothing burns like vanquished ambition.

When night arrives in starlit slippers,
be ready to dance like Mercury on a dime.

Application

Winner of the Golden Hind Award
Recent residency at Valhalla
Commissioned by Jove
Hungry for love's sawdust
Residency at Coconino County Jail
Guilty of being a judge

A stuffy taxidermist
Latest book: *Muffin Liqueur*
Never sorry for apologizing
Hornier than the brass section in a Marine Band
Hornier than a herd of longhorns
Hornier than Fashion Avenue at Rush Hour

A slender slander magnet
A dream runner in the fun brigade
Making room for emptiness inside

Hell´s Training Wheels

I suck so much I free the wind.
Pull words from its tailpipe.

In the junkyard
of beauty, I circle the wagons.

Barbie may be God's chauffeur
but I am his prince of ash.

I hunt the next breath
and chain it to the last.

Love is the only debt
I still have left. Emptiness

fills me with empathy.
In my genes, genies dream.

Fallen leaves, like
yellow teeth, grin at my feet.

Young Glove

Alone in the waiting room. Saying
adios to a molar going south.

December gutters like a candle.
The markets test the bottom.

I climb down from the wheelhouse,
reluctantly, to take my medicine.

Up to my neck in sunset.
The glove is not so young anymore.

Ivan Argüelles grazes
on his talking grave.

Did you see the Ski Jump?
Fast. High. Straight. True.

The new moon forklifts night,
giving us all the now time can handle.

Part II

Stretching Silence

Ali Baba's Last Alibi
or Bel Air

The ducks are sitting pretty today.
The sun plays peekaboo.
It's April. I love you like an iron
sinking into an iceberg. *Hiss.*

We know how to pump bliss.
How to praise our circumstance.
You bring me tea and hyacinths.
A fallen angel bakes us a cake.

I must arise and go now
to meet the Voidoids in the past
where a routine became a route
and a ghost became a guest.

Flip your turn signal on, babe.
Make a right to find what is left.

Pass It On

I am because we are.
—Senegalese saying

Dance daily with a broom.
Lead from the hip.
Wrestle with restlessness.
Put yourself on the map.
Seek a good-looking seer
to keep you stoked up.

Our partners are our armor.
They're the arms we bear
and have reason to cheer.
Red taillights smear
Avenue B's wet mouth.
Driving words into herds.

Guilty of touch.
Always dying just to be us.

Come On Now

Evening stoops under its sodden shawl.
A siren broods; its caterwaul
snarling over blackened roofs.
Someone's on the run.
Wet tires whisper to Avenue C.
"I'm lost without you," they swear.

I wanted to be a matador
in Manhattan, dancing with horns.
I wanted to be a genie
smoking in your coat of arms.
While you gave the raindrops names,
I made up a little song called

"You'll never be happier
than when I was a string on your harp."

Dalliance with a Dervish

Let's go to the used lingerie store and try some
on. Oh wait, that was a pastime from the past.
A spot of fun on love's cummerbund.

Night's menu no longer means you will come
to pass the time with me and my puppet crew.
As Ulysses said to Circe, yesterday fits perfectly.

When tears are delivered hot, the gondolier
speeds up but water remains unmoved.
Even Superman coughs, crooking his sleeve.

Recovery time varies depending on the variants.
We've had a good run on this little planet,
this remote outpost spinning in outer space.

Egad. The chits fall due. I'm out of milk
and cookies but I'm saving some hope for you.

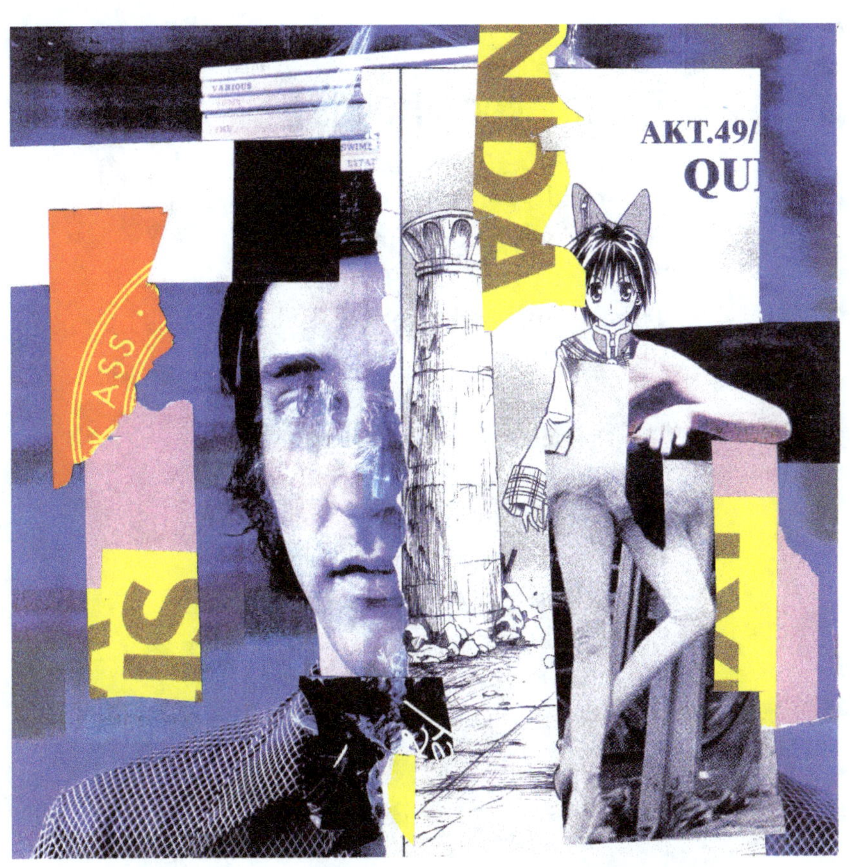
VARIOUS
K ASS
AKT.49/
QU

The Cuckoo's Holiday

St. Brigid's bell rings on Avenue B.
Holly waves hello from a garden.
"Winter's Dream" by Tchaikovsky plays.
Time's wingéd chariot races ahead
like the National Debt.
All I can say is CUCKOO!
'Tis the season to forgo regret
and pile love around the pilings.
Tangerines in hand-knit stockings.
Chocolate covered cherries for Dad.
White lace for Mom's dresser.
Let's get lost at my place
and count every pregnant hour.
Calling all angels—stand and deliver.

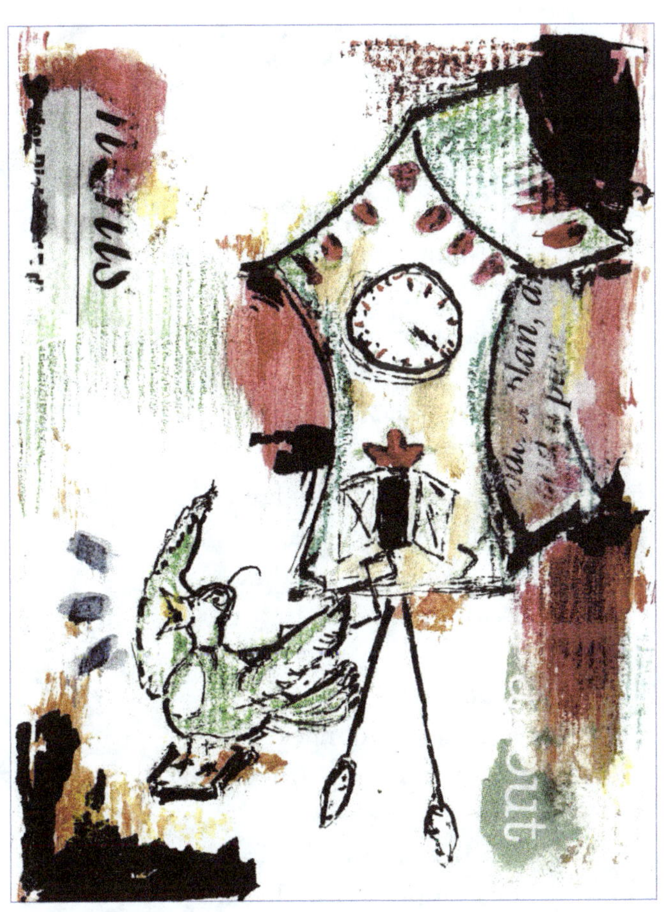

How Not To Do It

Never overplay your hand.

Dusting the Empire
with my feather boa . . .

what a drag it is—getting old.

Bound by Glory.

Cottonwood tufts land
on my black jeans.
Mud smudges one knee.
Praying can get dirty.

"The four-second pour
equals four ounces."
Every day is a learning day.

On Inkster Road going north,
I catch sky in my throat.

Waiting for UFOs

for Amy Barone

The main idea is to remain behind
after the dust clears

When owls hem night's gown

Rummaged by talking wind
Suddenly always

"You're a riot"
becomes an algorithm

FIRE SAIL

My only jail is pleasure

It's time to make something
that will last for all time

But it will take forever, you swear

Milking the dugs of divinity,
I fill drums with drops of infinity

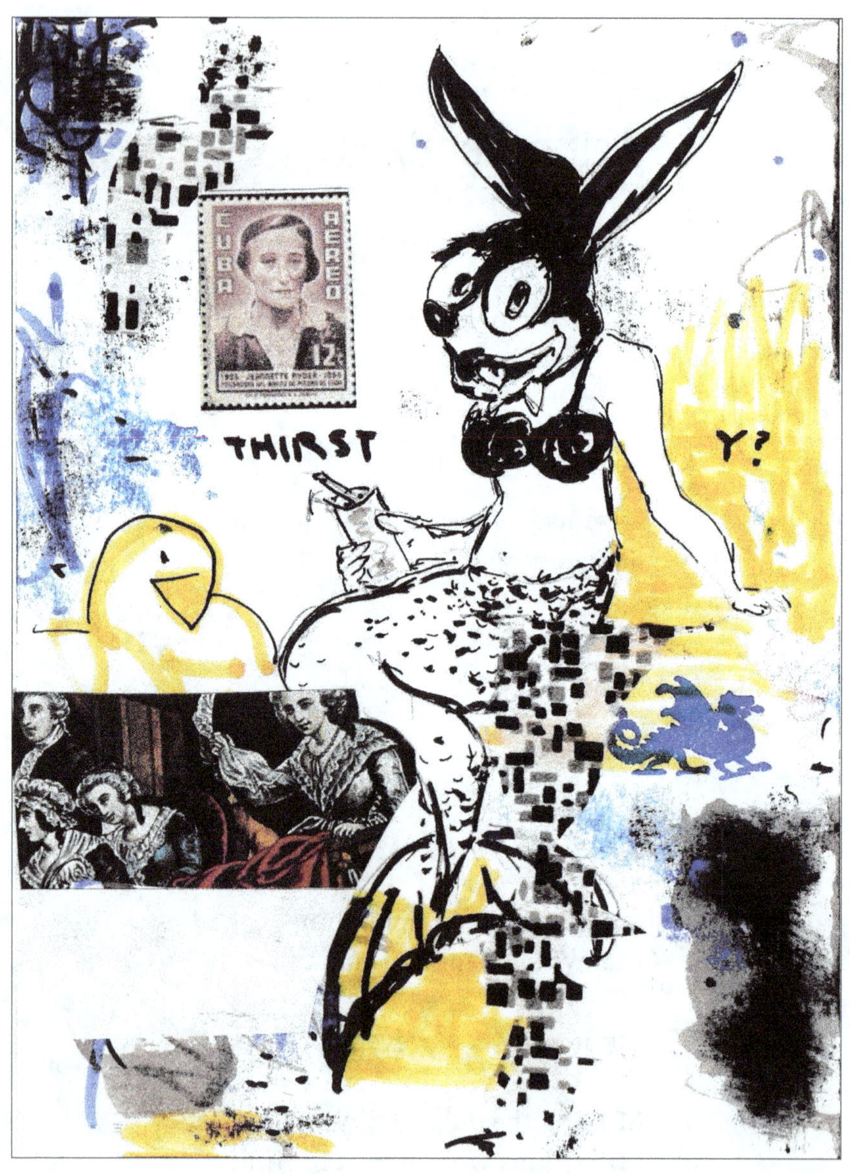
CUBA
AEREO
12
THIRST
Y?

Loosing It

The new moon—a hammer dent
on evening's chipped cupboard…
a wink at Mount Hood.
I have known you, little brother,
sixty years. We've gotten hammered
too, on white lightning and green.
You remember Grandma's jokes:

When the weather's hot and sticky,
that's no time to dunk your dicky.
When the frost is on the pumpkin,
that's the time for dicky-dunkin.

You are fire in a drum.
No one speaks ill of you.
How do you manage?
I open a letter from August.
Let us cast our nets into mad foam
and pull out the wishes of bones.

Required Fields

Clouds shuck the sky leaving pearl.
A Chinese woman walks a Welsh dog.
I am a swan and you are becoming
a ladder made of wands. We
believe in the Pirates of Penance.

Detectives search for a missing address.
Friends attend a random protest.
Some of us bet on long shots,
charting a course of emptiness.
Our shoes wear out chasing a dream.

Once, our eyes burned, torturing light.
Remember how we begged for answers?
Now catastrophes are nothing new.
Gratitude never ends. Other things do.

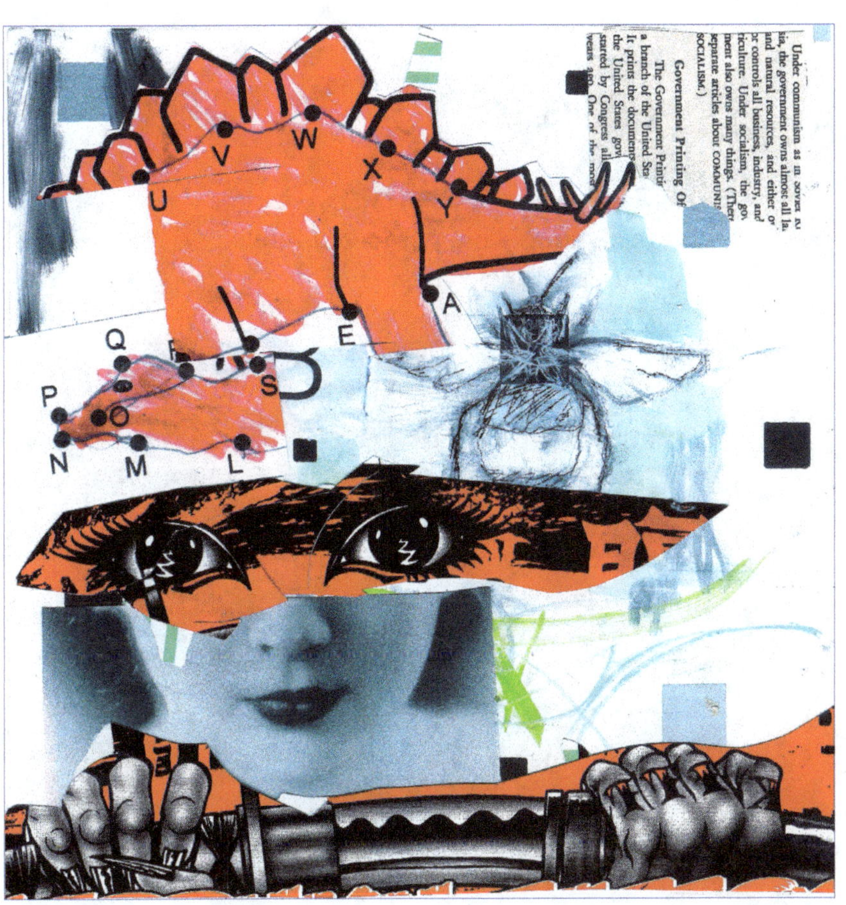

Under communism as in sovet
sia, the government owns almost all la
and natural resources, and either o
or controls all business, industry, and
riculture. Under socialism, the go
ment also owns many things. (Ther
separate articles about COMMUNI
SOCIALISM.)
Government Printing Of
The Government Printi
a branch of the United St
It prints the documen
the United States gov
started by Congress al
years ago. One of the mos

Ruby Lips

God's never in a hurry. Two girls
test young wind with a red kite.
Patience is your best friend.

Thunder cracks its knuckles and deals
from the bottom. All is for naughty,
my heart-piercing warbler.

You have perfected the purr.
It alone in your throat is pure
as if you were a big dipper
forever pouring star milk.

The window squints at grace.
And honey bees carry secrets
mouth-to-mouth, making
the trumpet vine's ruby lips gape.

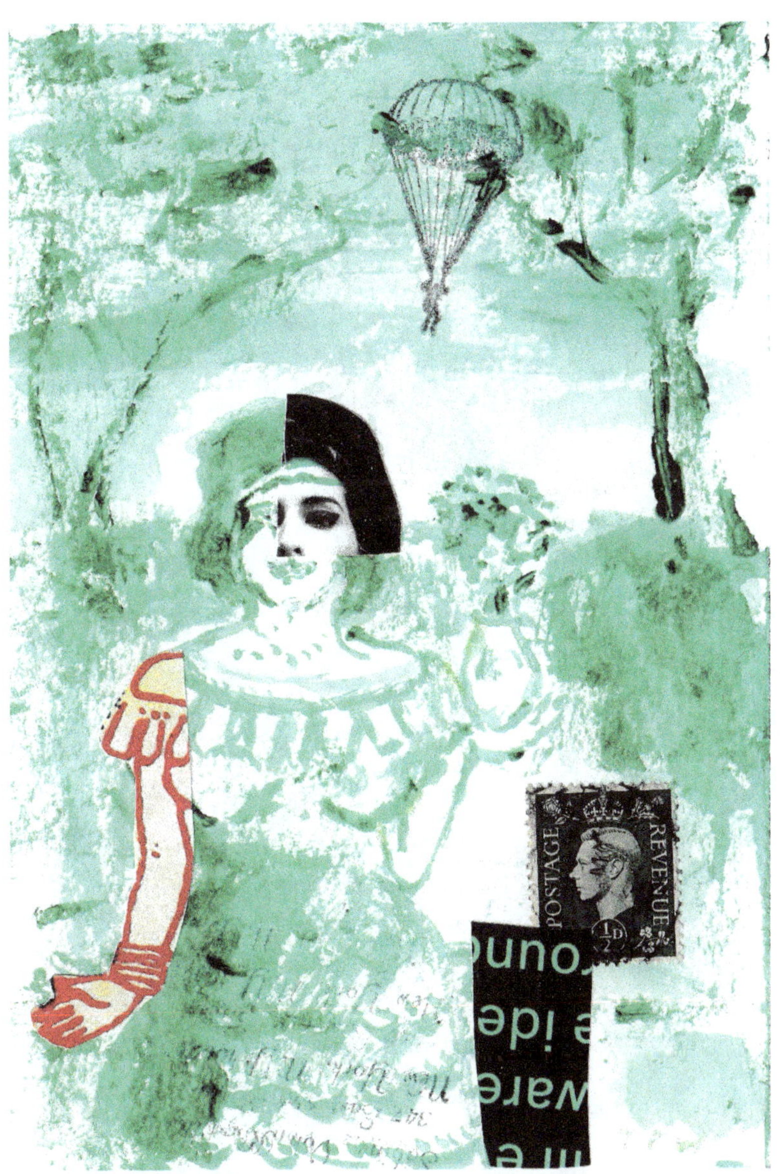

Shining the Moon

What is there to say about here?
—Elaine Equi

I've been awaiting
your ivory arrival—
your sickle smile.

Some bruised clouds
observe you warily
over Tompkins Square.

An earring on the sky.
White lashes
on a closed eye.

All my troubles
fall off their pedestals
when you come home

stretching silence
between thin horns.

Les Fleurs de Nuit

Dream I'm swimming with Ron
and smoking a j in the East River.
Dream I take too many silly pills.
I've lost my marbles, says Jennifer.

Dream I get to the airport on time
for a change but can't return the car.
Dream I back out of a bank robbery.
Dream I'm kidnaped by Circe's twin.

Dream you are a lady bug and I
am cowbane. Onyx spots on scarlet
wings, you search my upturned face.
We share an accident of grace.

Learn by doing—lead by dreaming.
Untie knots of wind by breathing.

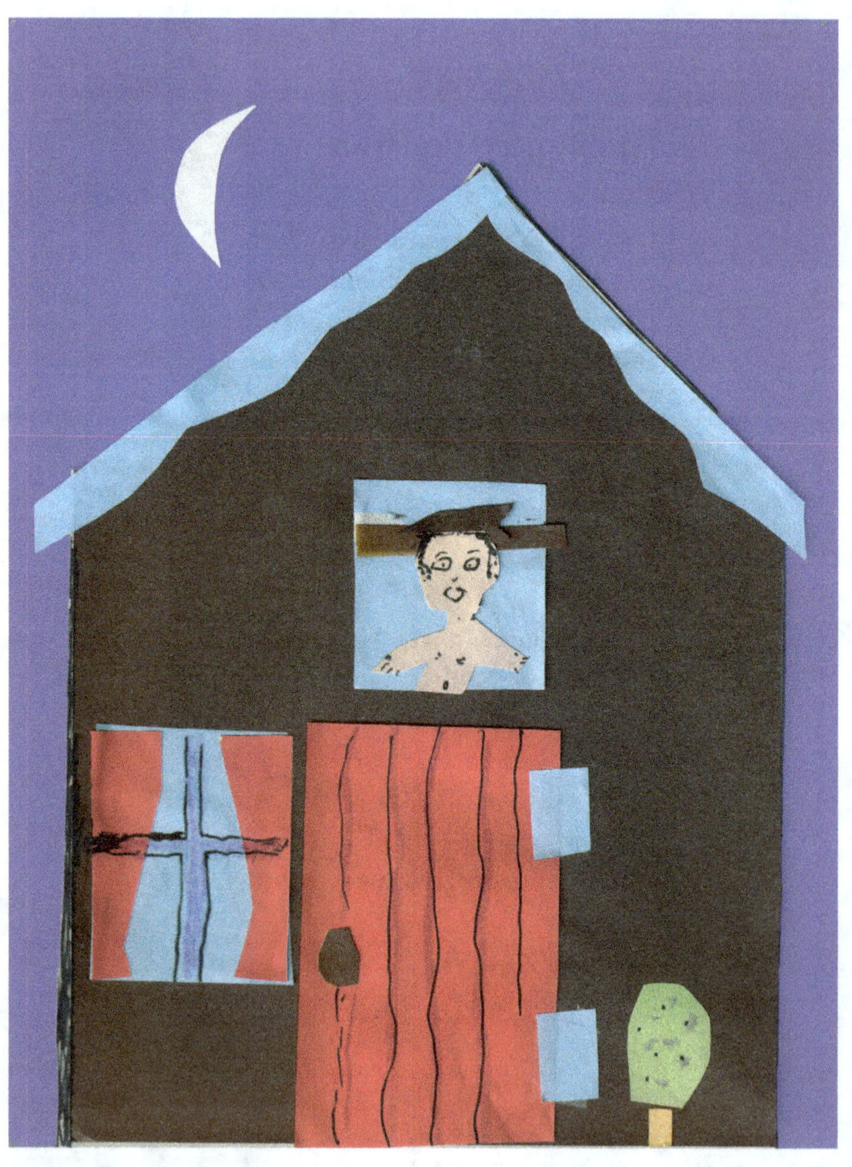

Shavings and Loan

Jump right in. What gives pause
is tomb-sweeping duty but duty
calls. Scramble the Phantoms.
What feels like 100 per cent is.

Maybe. Befuddled by fudge …
dithering and diddling. Fiddling
at the Fire Sale. Lonely
as a pangolin on the South Lawn.

Witness the witless grandstanding.
Inherit the bagged wind.
My spring is trying hard.
White buds flex perplexed resolve.

What dusk begins, dawn will erase.
Dear landlord. I rest my case.

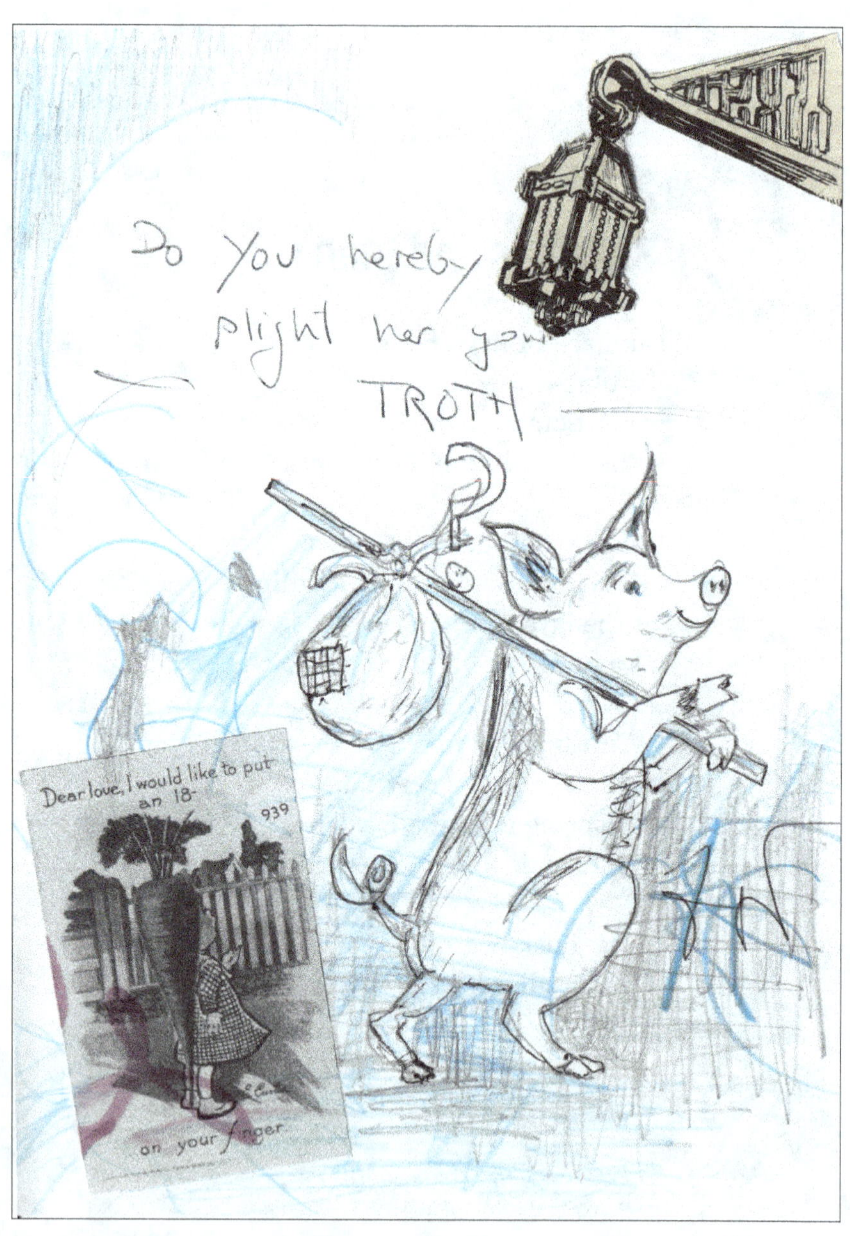
Do you hereby
plight her your
TROTH
Dear love, I would like to put
an 18-
939
on your finger.

Temporary Sanity

. . . forever in the sweat of fire.
—Philip Lamantia

Winter's white heart steams.
Venus pins night to the sky.
A few stars are hung out to dry.

On call at the dream hospital,
my gang of bells rings.

Me and you in the pitch light,
throb like a pulsar.
Listen. Your canals can hear
my eyelids beating time
into wings of gold foil.

All of what I say to you comes
with a moneyback guarantee.

And snow only really talks
when it starts to melt.

The Mystic's Mistakes

It wasn't until we left the casino
that I began Begging Lessons. Even

now, my lips won't speak to each other.
Trying to decide on sole or flounder.

The harbor sloshes in pearly galoshes.
The air, thick. The bathroom door sticks.

Tuesday relaxes in its smoking jacket.
Giving fire a haircut.

Listening to "The Cuckoo" by Respighi,
I depend on winks from the Sphinx.

All the chimeras dance to my tune
en route to the present tense.

Let us be measured by devotion.
NO VACANCY blinks in our vision.

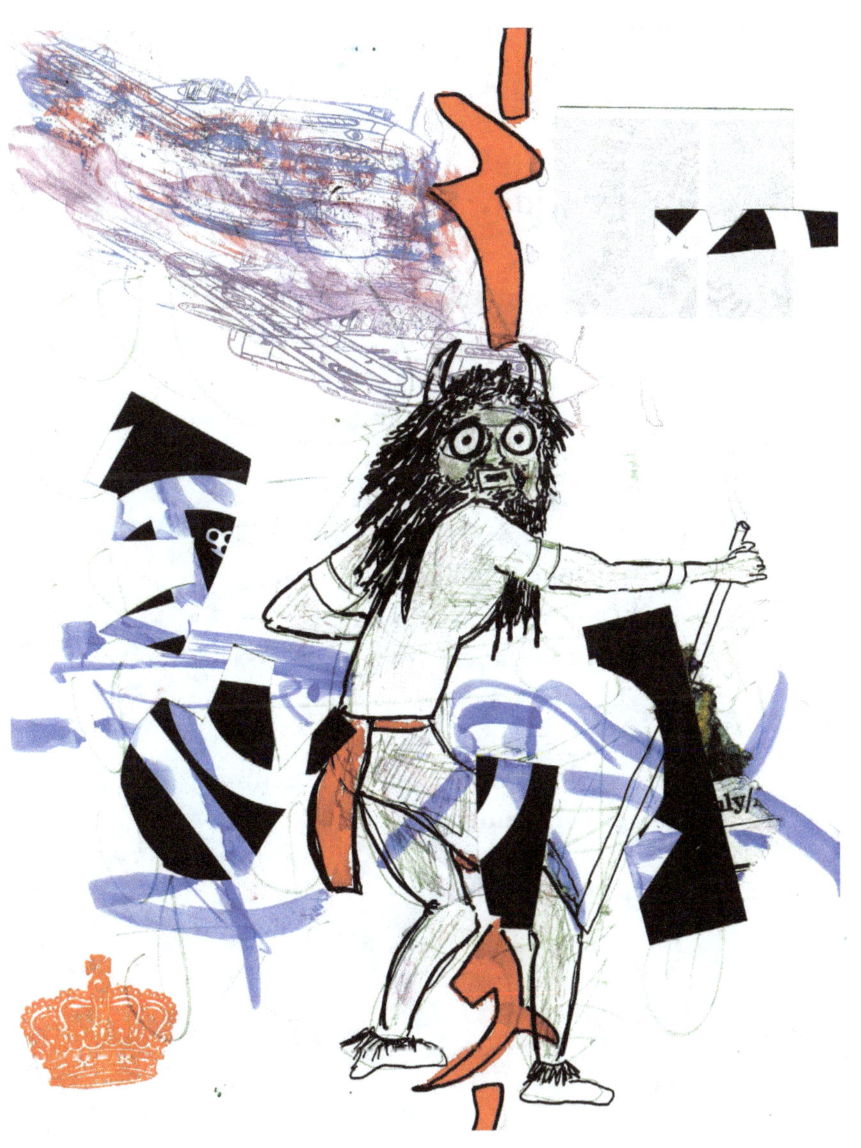

Go Big or Go Home

Would you rather be a mammoth
or a mastodon?
Let me think for a minute.
Let me be your mandate.
Let letters fly in pairs
around the spires of Paris.
Let my lips, two pilgrims blush
deciphering silence.
The souse shall rise again.
Let the leaders stonewall.
Let black sleet tuck night in.
Let life consume us,
a friendly fire licking the ceiling,
growing hungrier by the second.

The Auteur's Progress

The Cuckoo's Testimony.
The Cobbler's Soul.
The Hat-maker's Headache.
The Bell's Endless Toil.
The Witness's Falsies.
The Trunk Full of Peanuts.

The Secretary of Amnesia.
The Crabby Fiddler.
Salt's White Murmur.
Charlotte's Webinar.
Turning into Saturn.
Roasted Blue Inside.

You Are the One I Find.
Lost in a Desert of Light.

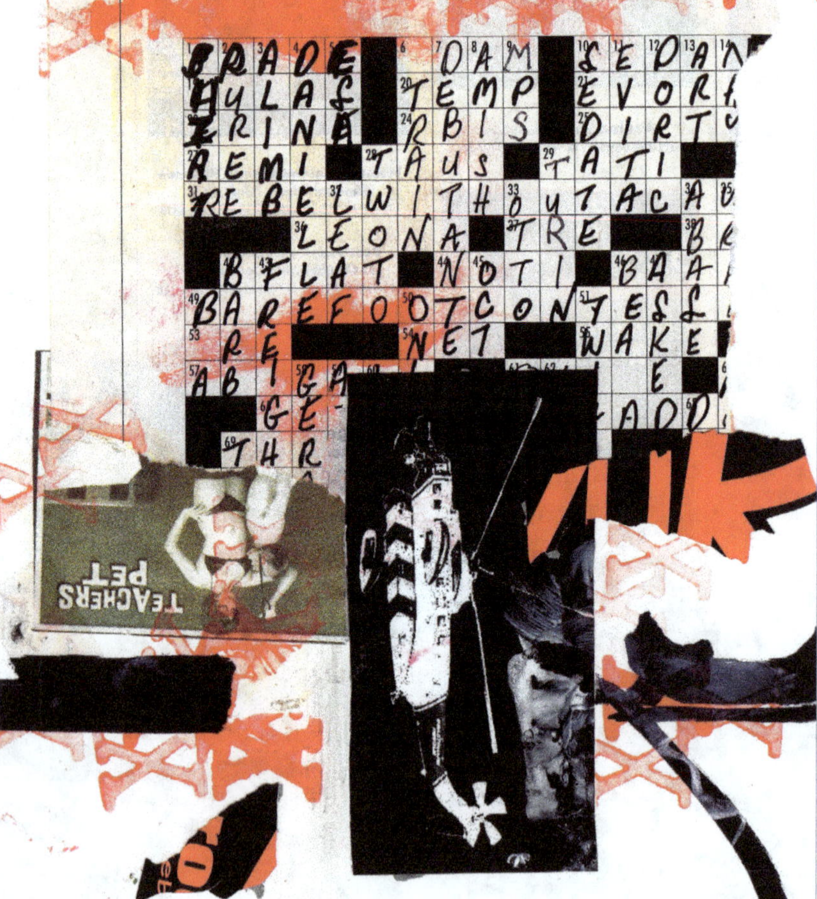
Crossword
The Have-Nots
New York Crossword by Maura B. Jacobson
TEACHERS PET

The Impossible Page

She's peeved. My wee granddaughter's
so transparent. Jealousy registers as
saucer eyes hogging the camera,
blocking out her little sister.
Her petulance at not getting a treat
is classic. Knocking over the tower.

The page too can be a terror—holding
its breath. Capricious. Demanding.
Not sharing toys. I've seen you
like that before, disguised as a star.
Ah, Venus. Take me away. Show me
where to aim. Courage let me wear.

Let's go to the pier and stare down time.
The sun is not the only thing burning.

By All Means

Even grass prays for meaning, each
blade marrying dirt and light.

The moon inches up, confessing
to both envy and lust.

We spoke for an hour
about giving ourselves assignments

without getting permission.
July. Persimmons out of season.

Red wine and blue smoke.
Steve Cannon has left the building.

The sky is lost in a purple robe.
The bells of St. Mark's give me a chill.

Grass rejoices when we come home.
And leaves applaud the wind.

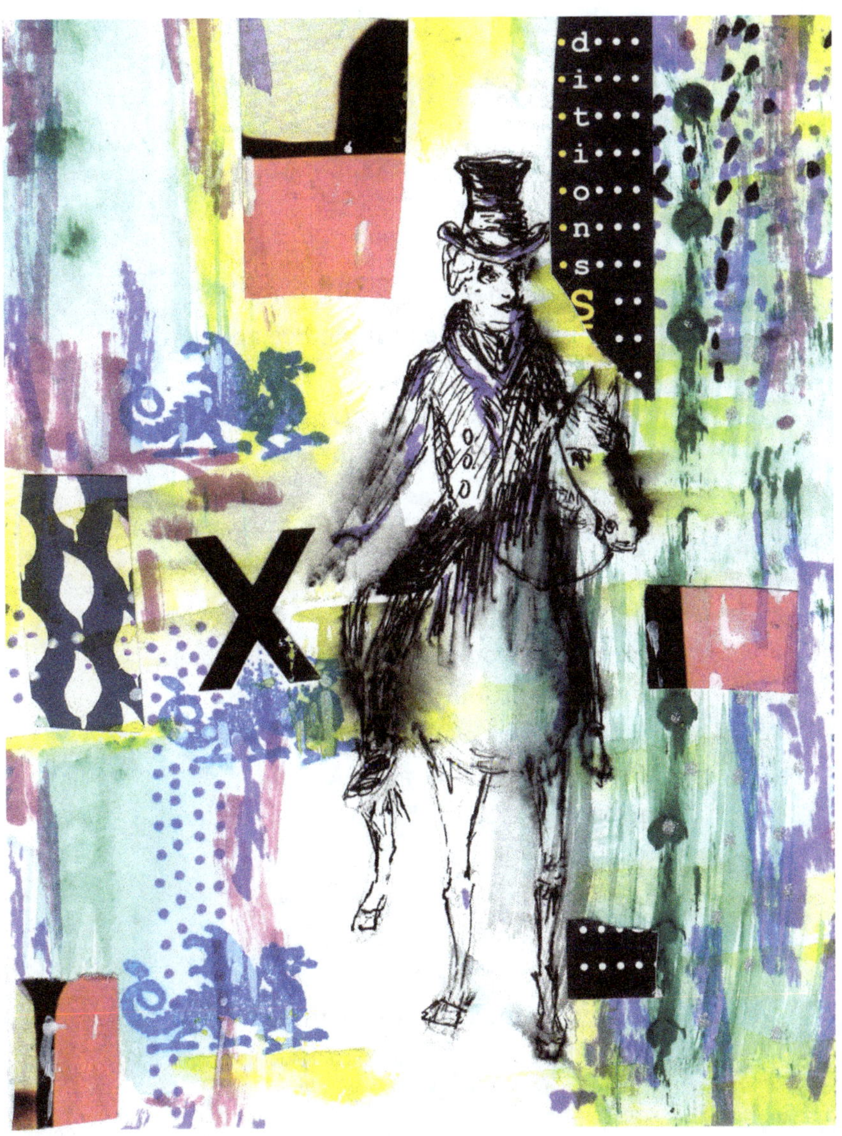
ditionsS
x

Blazing Stars

Force without mind falls from its weight.
—Horace

Mining for meaning amid awful loss,
we bid the humble bumble bee adieu.

Finding purpose in service I work
and live to give you a tumble.

We wake in this season of sleep,
swept forward toward a precipice.

America festooned in purple and black,
flags stick stubbornly at half mast.

Mad money incinerates our odds,
methane flares in the burn-off stacks.

Angel wranglers, use me for bait.
It's never too late to placate the gods.

Walk with me backwards into the fog
and rescue a tomorrow trapped by fate.

Echo's Chamber

Mutual love is the law of human life.
—Leo Tolstoy

A fat moon trundles across the sky,
a Mac truck with one headlight.

I sleep alone in night's salon
pining like a nut.

The only thing better
than one guitar is two guitars,

your sunglasses reflecting my eyes
in July's jonquiled haze.

Resistance is futile.
Whatever you say.

The DJ is my best friend.
Gulls laugh at love's slaughter.

I hear you rule with an iron caress.
My ears blaze in your absence.

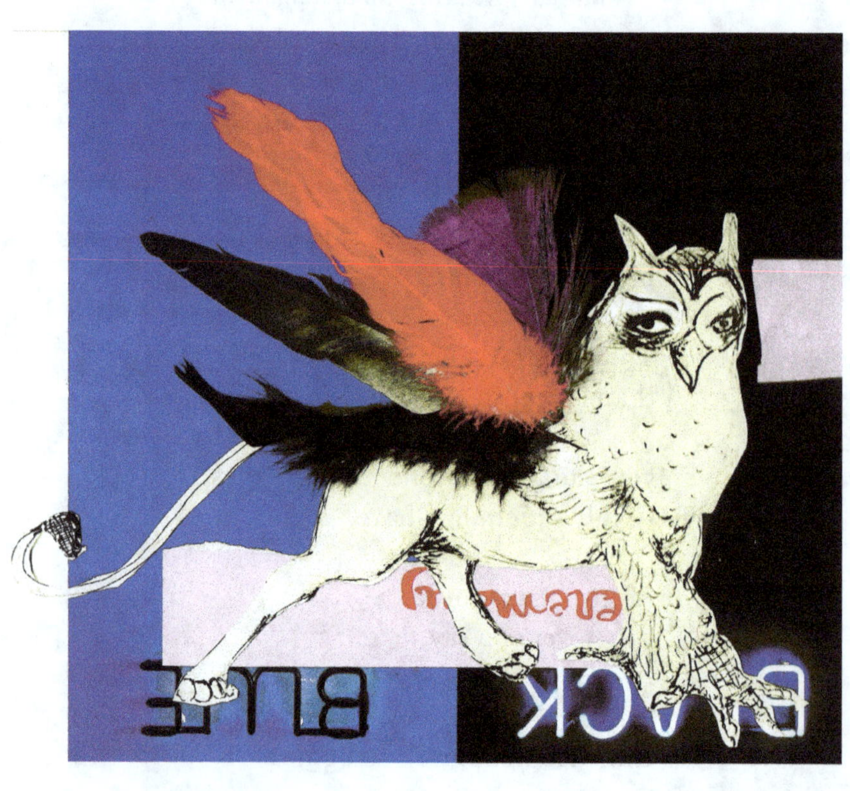

BLACK
BLUE

Burning Rings

Seven grackles tickle a hickory.
August unties its clown shoes.

On the thirteenth of evermore
in the year of nothing less,

I hold to you a blinding mirror
and you light me like a fuse.

Smell of old oaks in the park...
the ache of fading panache.

"Shut up and keep bailing,"
said the old salt to his mate.

You still look great
in the future we're creating.

Embers of a carousel, we are
burning rings, forged by stars.

Here for You

October lights a lantern in the aspens
under your window. The river unties
night's black ribbon and lies back,
eager to continue swapping whoppers.

After the yawning contest we'll put
the final touch on our opera bouffe
and bask in each other's wilderness.
Knockin' on the lockdown's door.

My puppets file for unemployment
and burn their orders from Moscow
Mitch. Lambaste the bastards.
Ok, who ordered the turkey cobbler?

I dream I drive an empty limousine.
There's a place here for you to fill in.

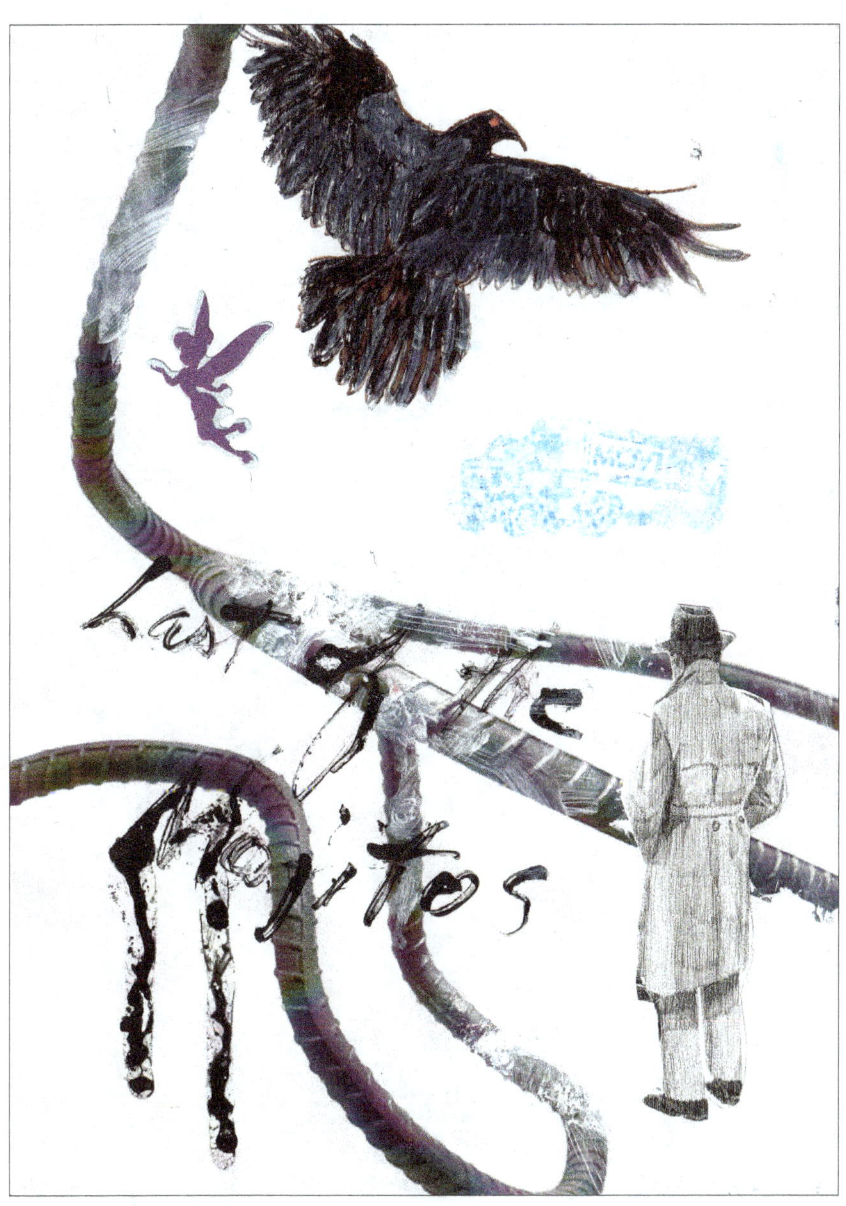
Last of the
Mojitos

Publication Credits

The author wishes to thank the editors of the following publications where some of these poems first appeared:

AMFM Magazine, Big City Lit, Big Hammer, The Brooklyn Rail, The Café Review, Clockwise Cat, Fell Swoop, First Literary Review East, Fjords, Hanging Loose, Hurricane Review, Live Mag!, Main Street Rag, New American Writing, North of Oxford, Poetry Bay, Poets Reading the News, Posit, Positive Magnets, and *Sensitive Skin.*

Purgatory Pie Press published "Make it Happen" as a letterpress hand-printed postcard.

Anthologies: Poems were included in *NYC from the Inside, NYC Throught the Eyes of the Poets who Live Here*, edited by George Wallace from Blue Light Press; poems and art were included in *Bordado de Voces (An Embroidery of Voices)* edited by C. D. Johnson; *Brevitas Annual Anthology of the Short Poem, 2017, 2018, 2019, 2020, 2021*, and *2022;* and *Contemporary Surrealist and Magic Realist Poetry,* edited by Jonas Zdanys.

Artwork was previously published in *Empty Mirror, Local Knowledge, Novostria!*, and *Poets Reading the News.* Artwork was previously shown at Theater for the New City, Tribes Gallery, and the Fountain Art Fair.

The author would also like to thank the hosts of several venues where these poems were performed: El Museo del Barrio, Howl! Happening, KGB Lit Bar, La Mama E.T.C., Lichtundfire Gallery, Mizuma and Kips Gallery, and Tompkins Square Library.

ACKNOWLEDGEMENTS

Special thanks to the following people who have been greatly supportive: Jane Friedman of Howl! Happening; William Electric Black and his *Poetry Electric* series at La Mama E.T.C.; Marc Vincenz for including me in the Surrealist Poetry Festival; Marc, Jonathan Penton, and Larissa Shmailo for including me in the Lit Balm reading series; Terence Winch for including a poem from *Blue Lyre* in *Best American Poetry.*

Thanks to James Feast for reviewing *Blue Lyre* in *The Café Review*; Sparrow for reviewing *Blue Lyre* in *American Book Review;* g emil reuter for reviewing *Party Everywhere* in *North of Oxford;* Greg Bem for reviewing *Party Everywhere* in *Rain Taxi;* Ilka Scobie for reviewing *Party Everywhere* in *American Poetry Review;*

Also, Alyona Glushchenkova, Luigi Cazzaniga, and the New York Public Library for producing the biographical film *Cuckoo O'Clock, Mr Underground—Jeffrey Cyphers Wright, Poet, Publisher and Impresario.*

Finally, additional thanks to Mark Ari, Rob Curcio, Joel Dailey, Linda Griggs, Ron Kolm, Steve Luttrell, John Reed, Barbara Rosenthal, and Barry Wallenstein. And to Lori Ortiz for her dedicated editorial assistance and design of *Doppelgängster.*

ABOUT THE AUTHOR

Jeffrey Cyphers Wright received his BA from West Virginia University and moved to New York City in 1976. He took workshops at the Poetry Project at St. Mark's Church in-the-Bowery with Ted Berrigan, Alice Notley, John Godfrey, and Jim Brodey.

He went on to receive an MFA in poetry after studying with Allen Ginsberg at Brooklyn College. For many years Wright taught at Brooklyn College and other institutions including the Poetry Project and Teachers and Writers Collaborative. He was awarded grants from Poets and Writers to teach and host events.

Wright founded Hard Press and published postcards by 100 different artists and poets along with five books, including the anthology *3-Zero, Turning Thirty*. From 1986 until 2001 he published 80 issues of *Cover Magazine, The Underground National*. The magazine was unique in its coverage of all the arts.

In 2007, Wright began *Live Mag!*, a journal of art and poetry. The publication has produced 19 issues. In addition to publishing, Wright is an impresario and regularly hosts art and poetry events. He's also an art and literary critic. For years he had a poetry column in the *Brooklyn Rail*. Currently, he reviews for *ArtNexus, Rain Taxi*, and *American Book Review*.

An eco-activist, Wright put his all into protecting community gardens. He produced a play and a film about his adventures. He has also made films using his poetry, puppetry, collage works, and grandchildren.

Poems have been published widely and are in several anthologies including *The World; Aloud, Voices from the Nuyorican Cafe; Thus Spake the Corpse, An Exquisite Corpse Reader; NYC Insiders*; and *Best American Poetry*. His artwork can be found online and has been shown at Tribes Gallery, the Manny Cantor Center, 532 Gallery Thomas Jaekel, the Fountain Art Fair, and other venues.

Wright has enjoyed residencies at Howl! Happening and eMediaLoft. He won a Theater for the New City poetry contest and he's a Kathy Acker Award winner for poetry and publishing.

www.ingramcontent.com/pod-product-compliance
Lightning Source LLC
LaVergne TN
LVHW020056110826
845155LV00022B/88

* 9 7 8 1 9 5 2 3 3 5 5 8 7 *